# Why are you my GRANDMOTHER?

Written by
## BRENDA SIRI
*Illustrated by Kristy Patterson*

Copyright © 2024 Brenda Siri
All rights reserved
First Edition

Fulton Books
Meadville, PA

Published by Fulton Books 2024

ISBN 979-8-89427-559-8 (paperback)
ISBN 979-8-89427-560-4 (digital)

Printed in the United States of America

*Dedicated to the sweetest boy on the planet, Kaeden Levi, who has forever changed his Gigi's life.*

My name is Kaeden and I'm 7 years old. One of my favorite people on the planet is called Gigi. That is her funny name she goes by instead of grandma.

I met my Gigi when I was one week old, but I don't really remember that. I just know that Gigi has always been in my life.

Gigi lives about four hours away from me, so I only get to see her every couple of months. When I go to her house, I get to fly on an airplane!

When I go to Gigi's house, we always have a lot of fun. We play a lot of games and go to the movies. And sometimes, we just sit together and snuggle.

I have a grandma where I live, and she is my mommy's mother. I see her a lot and she is a very special person in my life. When I was about five, I started to wonder who my Gigi really is.

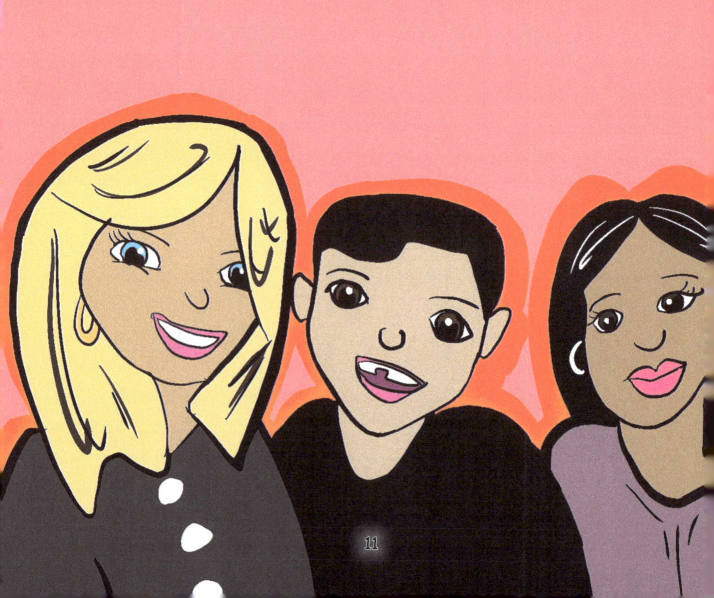

I finally asked my mommy and she told me that my Gigi is my other grandma. That made me feel really good, because having two grandma's is really awesome! It made me feel extra lucky!

When I was six, I started going to school. A lot of my friends only have a mommy like me, but there are lots of kids that have a mommy and a daddy. I've never had a daddy, so I started to wonder why I had two grandmas and a mommy, but no daddy.

First, I asked my mommy if I had a dad. She said that I do, but he was not ready to be a dad when I was born. I asked why because that made me very sad. She said that I should talk to my Gigi. I can talk to my Gigi about anything, so I asked her why.

My Gigi told me that she has a son who is my daddy and that makes her my grandmother. She said that my daddy has a lot of problems and was not ready to be a dad. She showed me this picture of her with my daddy so I would know what he looks like. I think we look a lot alike.

Then my *Gigi* told me the best thing ever. She told me that she loves me and that it makes her so happy to be my grandmother. I love her so much, too, and I am so happy she is my grandmother. Even though I don't get to see my dad, I have the best mommy and two really special grandmas.

Now I know why Gigi is my grandmother.

# About the Author

Brenda Siri is the president of an HR consulting firm. She is also an adjunct professor for The University of Texas at Dallas. Brenda is married with three children and two grandchildren. She is passionate about her family first, then her work, and her students. When Brenda is not working or teaching, she commits time to philanthropic activities. She also loves to travel the globe.

Brenda has a bachelor's degree in business and a master's degree in organizational management. She grew up in California but resides in Dallas, Texas, with her husband, Andrew, and their two dogs, Paisley and Khloe. Their children and grandchildren live nearby, and the family spends a lot of time together.

Printed in the USA
CPSIA information can be obtained
at www.ICGtesting.com
LVHW071636091124
796096LV00025B/263